**TASEREDGED
WATCHOUT!**

TASEREDGED
WATCH OUT!

tommy wyatt

Querencia Press, LLC
Chicago Illinois

QUERENCIA PRESS

© Copyright 2023
tommy wyatt

ISBN 978 1 959118 59 6

.
www.querenciapress.com

First Published in 2023

Querencia Press, LLC
Chicago IL

Printed & Bound in the United States of America

for fellow transmascs

"I'm mad! You fuck my life up, then you say, 'My Bad'"

You Make Me Sick! by Ashnikko

contents

content warnings

---

sexual situations, catfishing, CPTSD, ADHD, anxiety, dissociation, religious trauma, sexual assault, transphobia / anti- transmasculinity, body horror, boundary violation, alcohol use, drug use, parental abuse, self-harm, kink/bdsm, blood, child sexual abuse

trauma mapping + cptsd quiz *or a* letter to my last lover *or an* AI read *trick mirror or your computer screen*, and this is what it wrote

In 2009, I was catfished on MySpace, truly convinced I was dating an "emo hottie" because those who feel so wounded must be so, absolutely no reason at all to do it for "aesthetic" (that concept didn't exist then because if you look wrecked and vexed by an entire stick of black eyeliner, your peers may guess things about you, pound wounds out again [for 0, 1, 2, or 3 times? or more?], spitting in your mouth if you opened). And guess what? I wasn't talking to who I thought. Instead, a friend confessed. Did I mind? No, this had never happened before. So, I invited her over (in the summer). When she kissed my cheek, my whole body glitched technicolor and guylite.

Those feelings seared my brain *is to* fear as a personality trait? Because she broke her promise to be with me. (Is 12 too young to have amassed to [for 0, 1, 2, 3 betrayals?] [3^3, 3^6, 3^9 betrayals? or more?] Yet, in December 2010, I fell for another catfish, and at this point, I bet you're thinking "this is real silly" *is to* cooking fish to get the fishtaste out. This one was more famous, the similarities in names almost Electra complex-style, and I spoke in another language for (with?) him to only find some time later (in the summer), my boyfriend was a stan girl named D from somewhere else. She didn't know German really, which is why I had C's in *Intro to German*.

Are you still with me? I'm sorry. I know this is a lot already, if you count subtext. At the least, this was not the first time a friend was deliberate in manipulating me, I made it as easy as I'm making it now, telling you everything. (What you're not admitting now, but you could, is how you knew this already after you met parents. Now probably even more, and I don't understand this about them yet. If you tell me, would this break me as much or more than you planned to do? Which is better for you to choose?) Okay, okay. Thank you.

I'm sorry, but there's more. The next year, it's 2012, and I regrettably dated J. I'm reading these DMs from a deleted DeviantART account, telestless (autistic x ADHD crossover of echolalia shared with an ex-friend, but I didn't know this about me yet. I bet you're counting the times I say this [0, 1, 2, or 3?] [3^3, 3^6, or 3^9?] [6^3, 6^6, 6^9? or more?], huh?). Anyway, J played me (in the summer of 2012, from *The Hunger Games* to Goyte's "Somebody You Used to Know"). He mistook trauma (at first) for my identity, and really, I was convinced I needed to hold onto it to be a "real guy". I thought therapizing was true love because it's all I ever knew, because most people I crush on tend to date-to-save and discard when it gets boring. But I still hid things, I was never too open as J thought. I told him about K (told as in the context of vaguetweeting), and not D. But I told him I tried to kill myself by neglecting my health because that was how my parents loved me? Because I thought it would sound romantic to him?

Okay, that really was a lot now. I'm so sorry I said this. You're still with me?

When J claimed he studied my log-on patterns to DeviantART—what profile, for how long, what day of the week, and other measurements—so clinically, I told him:

> "account66 (think I have the username right) acts a lot like you with your 'nice face' on. I made this connection when we were still dating and it frightened me at the time because it seemed like you two were the same person. Clue # 2 could mean nothing or was that your confession of saying you're account66? Here I go again, figuring out these things. Ugh. Last time I did this I was right. Damn K..."

> A real message unarchived from an Internet grave I literally tried to bury digitally (or in real life, the difference doesn't matter here) and/or figuratively?

He responded:

> "Hey, you finally noticed. Good job. Although, I thought you'd pick up on it quicker. I even purposely slipped up sometimes to hint at it."

(After I tell you all of this, I'm crying, but you'll purposely slip into me. Proof to me that this is how to get attention I want when you're only proving this is how my attention serves you. I want it to be love, so I let you play tricks with my body, spitting in my mouth or moaning over the phone how you'd brutalize my hole. I want love so bad, I don't care about the cost, even if it's consent. Over and over again [0, 1, 2, or 3?] [$3^3, 3^6, 3^9$ times? or more?]. Did you know? If so, did you know that I am a body without boundaries? I know you knew something. You knew something the first night of August we met and you tried touching me, and after I took a hit so high I thought I'd impress you (I think it did, too well), I let you. Is that what you knew? That I'd always let you?

In 2023, I'm in therapy. Guess what? I have ADHD, too. I'm on Strattera, and I get high every night just like you did at 25. I still can't give consent sober because of you, and I get high to hunger, even through the night lunging to lilac.)

results

Scales on the 0 - 3 range fall under: **Possibly Likely**

Scales on the $3^3 - 3^9$ range fall under: **Highly Likely**

Scales on the $6^3 - 6^9$ range fall under: **Highly Likely**

my go-to text when i'm spiraling out of control

when i hallucinate, i often feel bugs crawling on my skin but every so often i get these ones that are just strange sensations i worry are something specific and it physically felt like skeleton bone but knew that couldn't be possibly realistic like i'm at a home, i'm not in the middle of a fresh plot in a graveyard, i'm not like my father who lived at the family cemetery when he was in his twenties so why would i ever think like that but i'm pretty faded and mentally ill so idk horror movies kind of start happening like this, almost like i'm awake during a nightmare, and the other night i hallucinated for the first time since i lived with my parents so badly it was like i was watching skinamarink which is why that movie was scary to process sober, and i really want to hurt myself sometime and watch it fucked up like this

how do i get my voice back? / when i *was* buffy, i was saying i'm a girl with my whole chest

FADE IN:

INT. TOMMY'S DREAM — TIMESTUCK IN A TIMESUCK

The moon shines too bright in TOMMY'S eyes, it's like they're bedazzled or something. That image sifts in THE GENTLEMAN'S mouth, swishing it around to get a good taste: husky in the way it stiffens the throat with notes of desperation. Twinkling on the tongue, THE GENTLEMAN licks his teeth with it, as his mouth silvers to a smile, like a steely *shinnnng* to knifebright smirk.

THE GENTLEMAN hovers above spikes of fake grass, a field of absence. No stars in the night, no exit signs. THE GENTLEMAN materializes anyway and always. The stark black, an expanse or a cage? Does it matter? When TOMMY—

FADE OUT:

OUTSIDE — ON CAMPUS / HIDING SPOT — NIGHTTIME

YOU and TOMMY are making out, so much that it steams up the church's porch light. Turns it orange. There is an abrupt pause that lasts maybe six seconds, but it should feel like it takes up more space than just that.

YOU
Where did you go? Your eyes went bright, like cartoon-stars when the dude's about to pass out.

TOMMY
Does it matter?

YOU
It doesn't ever with you. It makes you the perfect girl.

TOMMY
You really mean that?

TOMMY blushes amber from a skyward glance. The moon works in his favor.

YOU flash a smile and hold it for an uncomfortably long time without breaking. YOU mean to say something without saying it.

10 years later, i am haunted when i remember parawhore was my Kik handle in 9th grade

punch away the minutes with clicks of Snapchat messages
        (nobody dared me to commit to the bit
        but let's be honest about what i'm
        doing here)
i'm so soaked through and twitching, thinking about you kissing me, time
emitting the slow reverberating static with each ping.
        you are typing...

        "can i see your pink lips"

        (note: your message missed mentioning
        anything about how i confessed
        to blasting Paramore's unreleased cover
        of "Stuck on You" when i am haunted
        by nightmares of older others undressing
        my body as if i asked for it,
        they went after it anyway, much like you're doing now)

warped by the feeling i can fill a need, i unclench a little until
        you are typing...

        you send a gif of lips spreading,
        blearblinking like a bubble wand.

the last time i expressed interest in sex, you refused to fuck me because you said those who like BDSM deserve to be raped, and since then you've been true to your word

IT HAPPENED when the night atrophied, the sun digested a disgusting phlegmyellow, and spit up mustard sillystring clouds like confetti or glitter: it's everywhere, and it won't come out.

I never slept. How could I? You crinkled your body under your cumcrusted covers and ate me out, licking *everything*—to taint and beyond—as if you're trying to devour me whole.

It happened again with my eyes open, ashamed. I asked you why, and you said to sit back and relax. "You'll like it. All men do."

"you both watched *Fresh* (2022) on Hulu and *You* (2018-) on Netflix"

tommy

[fakeginger femme, splotched with mousy brown freckles under my left eye. not the cute kind, no. it may secretly be a face tattoo, and you'll lust over ripping my skin clean off, fingering the fresh red space to your cold and soiled knuckles until you twist your hand in deep, deeper, deepest. and you pull out the fleshiest sound, losing yourself to the stringy sinews that you pretend are *fruit by the foot* you won't fully chew, savoring it in the most intimate way you know how.

don't get lost in the details, there's more! my eyes are blank blue, or maybe they're just green but appear blue from a mysterious redness you hope is from a vision of me finally knowing you, one day.]

 25   5'4"   in a body stuffed with straw, bloated so bad like that hyperpop song you hatefuck your ex to. i will let you haunt me if you want, or raw me down until i'm good as a sack of meat cryptorotting in your freezer. there's always more of me to forget about.

what i'd like to know most about you
if you swipe right without reason, say so. what is it about me? i bet you crave scratching at my skin so hard, the fibers jam all the way up your nail beds. having a taste of me for, maybe, six months if you're lucky? do you think i'm game, is that it? just because i wanted a concept of you so bad once, which, for the record, was *way* before i knew the reason you swiped right was my set location. i wanted a hookup and a simple ghosting after. why is that so hard to find?

an email to you in business casual

Let me make it clear that my distance is a direct result of you crossing boundaries on multiple occasions.

I'm not sure why you keep ignoring my boundaries by creating new social media accounts (after I've blocked you on your other ones), or emailing me after I've blocked you, or asking to connect on LinkedIn (really?).

If you're lucky, I am thinking to hear you out, but I may choose to keep up taseredged boundaries. I need you to respect that.

shopping bag meets pop art meets popup message meets breadfish

when you want to screw someone(thing) in every state, why not do it in two with a shopping bag busting with condoms? why don't you spit in it, in me? as much as you lick your whippets (though i bought them hoping you would get me so high, but not when you handed me ecstasy) clean, chasing pathetically charged dopamine that'll burn up the next time we fuck in PA then the city. you remember the one, and we were so very inspired, thank you for that. in fact, this poem is because of you, or in spite of you, and no you cannot choose.

you want to screw me over? spit where you lick it? don't you know that will leave me crying at a gas station and sending you a blueyeshadow and tearstricken selfie on Snapchat, tits out (a little too risqué for this risk i know), and you haven't seen it for so long we lost our streak, and i dream of you telling me you wouldn't even want to touch me through a shopping bag, when how can that be true? when you shoved your cock (sans condom???) in my holes any chance you got?

any chance you remember how much sangria i drank, how soft and fuzzy i spoke, the possessed blearing of the eyes? or how a cuspid of light pierced them (it's cupid szn) i knew i wanted to love you? even when you left me in the hotel the night after we first really fucked, and we both cried, and you said no one has ever listened and i begged you not to leave. maybe it means something that this poem is because of you, or in spite of you, because i'm really trying to understand.

333 AITA for asking this question to this absolute downbad slutty catboy i'm talking to?

I think people come into my life for a reason. Wait, let me start over, I (27M) sexted T (24M?). T said it was "out of the blue" and questioned my motives, which I thought was really weird since he said he'd go back to the closet for me, put on an angelbaby and pewter cloud mesh top, tits out (I asked, what a slutty sub, amiright?). All I could think about was how sexy he'd look with a collar. Mm. A sexy little catboy. I'd fuck him into liking it, I knew I could.

Anyway, I wanted to know how far I could take this. I read one of his poems where he begged to be a fucktoy, nothing but holes desperate to be filled. I knew I got this, but he was needy in a way I don't have capacity for. My dick went weak when he said he did something he shouldn't have after emotionallyedging me with his trauma. (Edging me off a fucking cliff, amiright?) Something was "fileting his skin open", I mean, okay. He didn't say it like that, in a hazy glimpse I sworn I saw it. He said that he cut himself. Basically. I ignored him for a whole day, and sluts hate that. (Sluts hate this one trick!, amiright?) They ALWAYS come crawling back for this dick.

When he asked, "What are your intentions with me?", I fucked him so hard over texts and my softdom dares. So, next level, I asked: "Are you at the point where I'm able to fuck you? Fuck you in a hotel room on my ex's credit card, fuck you till your parts are spent?"

I haven't heard from him since, and I can't stop thinking about how he was immediately suspicious of me, but they say that kind of thing is a reflection on the other person, not me! So, I don't know, and I really miss those catboy titties. Am I the asshole?

1.5k comments   Share   Save   Hide   Report

28

YTA. Reading this was like losing myself in the pixels of each TikTok that stitches in my skin and skitters through the eyes, like how my eyes will fall asleep like a limb, gutting pixels out of the phone screen. My head splits like a pumpkin in claymotion movement, the pulp smacks inside my skull until it spelunks down my throat.

I told you I don't swallow.

I mean.

I want to say something else. Something you would understand. You know who this is. You told me all about your "kinky" Reddit name, and this display of humiliation is the kinkiest you could ever hope to be. I still think about what you said about your hands, how you wish you would grab me by the hips and shove your dick inside me if I agree to wear a blindfold, all "*Fifty Shades of Grey* style" (seriously?). Only because the thought is a moribund trespasser that'll risk nightmares. Too bad for me, huh? Too bad for me that your text settled into my stomach now, my brain fizzing and popping. I feel like soda was dropped on my head, if my head were a motherboard.

This is another way to say that I woke up from 44th nightmare about it, about what you said before. This was from a whiplashwarm nap in spongey pad of sun. In this new haunting, you lurked in the abyss of my unfinished basement, your hands cobwebcold, grizzled, and gray, lunging to me in puncturedflashes because I'm dissociating even here, and suddenly you've sunk your jagged nails in my hips, your wrist cracking like a glowstick. I woke up and felt your touch. I still do, and this was weeks ago. Why weren't you honest with me? Why didn't you say when I asked what your intentions were with me, you said "Just wanted to see what you were up to." Quickly followed up by a detailed instruction manual on how you'd like to fuck me in a cheap motel.

Comment

you said your breeding kink and my need for guided meditation should link up. did you even think?

	missive	liminal
sub	*imagine a mountain,* whirrs on the tape ringing with static. it's costumed with steely chainmail, reminding me how you feel about me bottoming.	the session tricks me when the cliff shifts to one from *Eden Lake.* where you are tossing me barbed wire as a rope to climb with, and i am not begging for you to
trans	say only if i wear a collar, so cold it silvers skin, and if i plump in thigh-high tights in fishnets, did you say you wish i was more femme, like you? is this your way of fucking me to a new identity?	say sorry this time in lightwork so liminal that fairylights twinkle in sootsmoked pittsburgh nights. and if i open my eyes, i'll know that it happened.

questioning your faith? (watch out!)

gender doesn't mean i'm your bro you can fuck,
and say "no homo" after (with sincerity). dude, i literally
sucked your cock with slipperyslick tongue, so
sleazy and sloppy like you asked, like you fantasized
about when you touched yourself in the shower with
water beading on your body in 2000s technochrome
slowness (time stills when you cum to me, how could you forget?),
like when you knew i was so high i gripped
onto your bathroomsink (covered in coarse and blunt curly
brown hairs) because my throat felt weirdly warm
and scratchy and you even admitted you knew right then
you wanted to put your cock in my mouth, just a little,
just to say you did, and just because i'm not a guy to you
when you bite off my mesh thong this night (or the next throng
of nights) frightened by pussy in a Biblical sense, like
pussy is a Biblically accurate depiction of an angel to you,
and while you want to be saved, maybe not like that and
not by that *thing*. but we're gazing into each other
for proof we want to be here as you pretend to christen
me over and over. with cum, seriously?

brr (why don't you take it out on me?)

i don't think you understand. how filthy i want
you to poke
and probe my hole and leave me with a soggy
frothed up white load
and tell me i deserve it. i think you'd rather eat soap,
the blockchalkiness purifying you a little too well,
because when i ask you to tell me the most disgusting
fantasy with wild abandon, you say you want to rub
your cock on any part of my body. i'm sorry
but what? fucking what? you have a piss kink and this
is the wildest thing you can think to ask for?
i am giving you permission to objectify me,
i'm telling you how sexy you look with your hair pushed back,
outlined by the raspberry red of streetlights against the nightsky,
and the only thing you muster is that you think it would be nice
to touch my pussy with your cock because it's a novelty?

just admit you won't fuck me like one of the boys
because all you see is a body with more holes than you're used to,
and you know what? you're so fucking boring for that.

imagine a man with the trauma of a teenage girl
subtitle: i exclaim! to myself! wow, *tommy's body?*

isn't it romantic if you whine
how you'd eat me: like
licking molasses
reaching for canned cranberries
that jiggle supple and soft, its skin pockmarked too, and look
how quickly russet shifts to sunset, sloshing in the body,
how you fantasize about my *fat titties*,
breathysighing at the end of the song? or is it the birthday
pasties i'm upset about? maybe you actually remembered
me saying something this time, saying how i think nipples
are useless on men. i think you said *a guy with a pussy is the ultimate slut*,
but in a way that makes me feel desperate, lucky for it,
when i'm really just relieved i only turn 27 once.

thank-yous and acknowledgements

Thank you to the following: Theo Sebastian, nat raum, Annie Morris, Alan Sachs, Magi Sumpter, charlie perseus, arden will, dre levant, and Katharine Blair for your friendship, guidance, and support. Thank you, as always, to my cats: Peanut, Mimi, Cosmo, and Skitty.

In "how do i get my voice back? / when i was buffy, i was saying i'm a girl with my whole chest", there is a reference to a *Westworld* episode (Season 3, Episode 3: "The Absence of Field") that references Mark Strand's "Keeping Things Whole" poem. The title of "brr (why don't you take it out on me?)" is a reference to "brr" by Kim Petras.

Thank you, nat raum, for your guidance, as always. Thank you, Emily Perkovich, for championing this book.

"trauma mapping + cptsd quiz or a letter to my last lover or an AI read *trick mirror or your computer screen*, and this is what it wrote" in Graphic Violence Lit

"imagine a man with the trauma of a teenage girl" in Passengers Journal

"you both watched *Fresh* (2022) on Hulu and *You* (2018-) on Netflix" in *NOW THAT'S WHAT I CALL HORROR!* through Gutslut Press (October 2023)

about the author

tommy wyatt (he/they) is the author of *NOW THAT'S WHAT I CALL HORROR!* (Gutslut Press, 2023), *So, Who's Courage?* (Bullshit Lit, 2023), *take this quiz! 11 questions to see if you agree with courage as a metaphor* (Ghost City Press, 2023), and several chapbooks. He thanks his cats—Mimi, Cosmo, Peanut, and Skitty—for late night interventions.

scan me to listen to the
TASEREDGED spotify playlist

ALSO BY THE AUTHOR

JETTISONED by what glows when you're in the closet (again) *(self-published, 2023)*

NOW THAT'S WHAT I CALL HORROR! (Gutslut Press, 2023)

take this quiz! 11 questions to see if you agree with courage as a metaphor (Ghost City Press, 2023)

So, Who's Courage? (Bullshit Lit., 2023)

that makes two of us (co-authored with Theo Sebastian; kith books, 2023)

space cowboy on a little, uh, space exploration? (Bottlecap Press, 2023)

nosedive & the mirror (self-published, 2022)

lacuna (kith books, 2022)

Peanut [the cat] auditions as Courage [...from Courage the Cowardly Dog] (self-published, 2022)

after: transience, transference, transfusions, & transmutations (self-published, 2022)

Trick Mirror or Your Computer Screen (fifth wheel press, 2022)

self-portrait as poems about bad poetry (self-published, 2021)

swerve (ELJ Editions, Ltd., 2021)

MIXTAPES (ELJ Editions, Ltd., 2021)

www.ingramcontent.com/pod-product-compliance
Lightning Source LLC
Chambersburg PA
CBHW061329120626
46546CB00007B/2733